the FRUIT FLIES' PICNIC

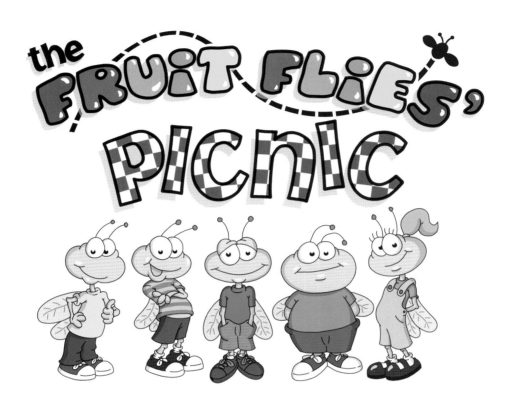

By Kathleen Stefancin, M.S., R.D.
Illustrated by Kirk Werner

Smart Picks, Inc., P.O. Box 771440, Lakewood, Ohio 44107

Or visit:

www.smartpicks.com

ISBN 0-9764785-0-1

Library of Congress Control Number: 2005900440

Copyright © 2005 by Kathleen Stefancin
All Rights Reserved. Self published by Kathleen Stefancin.

Printing by Amica Inc., Seattle, Washington
First printing, March 2005

Printed in China

Book design, cover art and all illustrations by Kirk Werner

For my mom and dad, who have always supported my creativity and encouraged me to write.

—K.S.

For my wife, Pam. Thanks for your never ending patience and tolerance. You're a Peach!

—K.W.

Deep in the forest, five playful fruit flies are preparing for a very colorful picnic.

Once the picnic table is set, the fruit flies will scurry away and bring back their favorite fruits.

"Here I come!" Gracie yells as she sets her plump red strawberry on the table and flies away. She waits for the others to bring their fruits.

"Look out below!" Zak shouts as he lets go
of his yellow star fruit.

"Here we go!" Ben sings as he opens his arms
and drops his green Kiwi.

Yum . . . yikes . . . yeekes! "This is fun!" Jake says as his cherimoya slowly bounces to the middle of the table.

Yippy . . . yea . . . yahoo! "We're almost done!" Nicholas shouts as his blueberries whirl through the air.

As the last blueberry lands on the table, the fruit flies race to their seats. There is an excited silence. Each fruit fly will take a turn and share something about the fruit they brought.

"Let's begin," Gracie says, holding up the red strawberry.
"You can eat the tiny black seeds on the outside."
Each fruit fly takes a bite.

Gracie tells her friends that red fruits help keep their hearts strong and their memories sharp. As she speaks, the fruit flies eat the whole berry and giggle as the juice tickles their tongues.

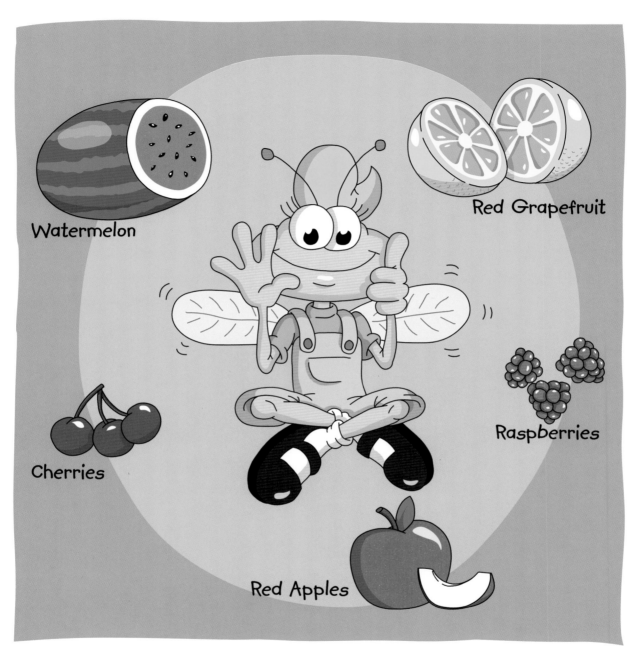

Watermelon

Red Grapefruit

Cherries

Raspberries

Red Apples

Gracie asks her friends if they can name five more red fruits.

Can you name five more red fruits?

Next, Zak picks up the shiny yellow star fruit. It twinkles in the sunlight as the tart brown seeds fall to the ground.

Delighted, the fruit flies finish every shiny, starry bite,
knowing that yellow and orange fruits help keep
their hearts strong and their vision clear.

Zak asks his friends if they can name five more yellow or orange fruits.

Can you name five more yellow or orange fruits?

Now it's Ben's turn. He holds up the fuzzy, brown-skinned kiwi. Inside, bright green fruit surrounds a circle of black seeds.

"Green fruits help keep our vision clear, and they also make our bones and teeth strong," Ben says. Thrilled, the fruit fly friends gobble up the rest of the green kiwi.

Green Apples

Green Pears

Avocados

Grapes

Honeydew Melon

Ben asks his friends if they can name five more green fruits.

Can you name five more green fruits?

Then Jake picks up the heart-shaped cherimoya. Most of his friends have never seen this fruit before. "White, tan and brown fruits also help keep our hearts strong," he says.

Jake splits the fruit in half and tosses the toxic black seeds on the ground. The fruit flies taste the creamy, white fruit inside. The familiar flavors of pineapple, papaya and banana surprise them.

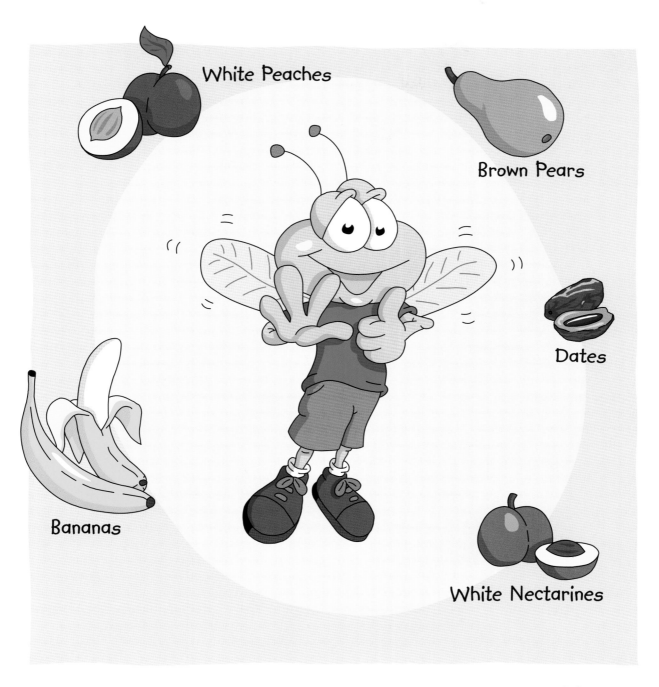

Jake asks his friends if they can name five more white, tan or brown fruits.

Can you name five more white, tan or brown fruits?

Finally Nicholas shouts, "Look! There's a star on top of the blueberry. If you touch it, a blue star will appear on your finger." Soon all the flies have stars on their fingers.

"Blue and purple fruits help keep our memories sharp and our bodies healthy as we grow," Nicholas tells them. Happily, the fruit flies eat the stars and then devour the entire berry, including the tiny seeds.

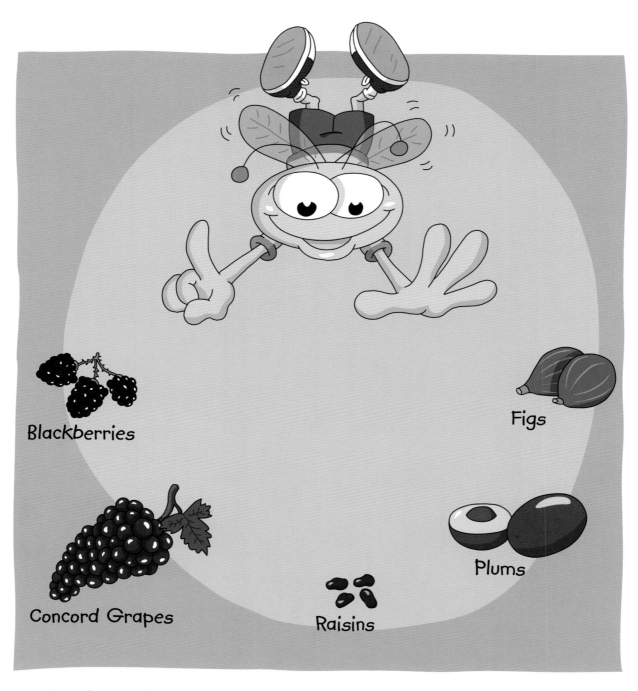

Blackberries

Figs

Concord Grapes

Raisins

Plums

Nicholas asks his friends if they can name five more blue or purple fruits.

Can you name five more blue or purple fruits?

By now, the flies' tummies are full of fruit and their cheeks
are full of smiles. They relax and think about all
the different colors of fruit.

Together the friends have tasted a red strawberry,
a yellow star fruit, a green kiwi, a white cherimoya,
and a handful of blueberries.

They have learned which colored fruits keep their hearts strong. Can you name the colors?

Red, Yellow and **Orange, White, Tan** and **Brown**

They remember which colored fruits keep their memories sharp. Can you name the colors?

Red, Blue and **Purple**

They see which colored fruits keep their vision clear. Can you name the colors?

Green, Yellow and **Orange**

They know which colored fruit makes their bones and teeth strong. Can you name the color?

Green

They are glad these colored fruits keep their bodies healthy as they grow. Can you name the colors?

Blue and **Purple**

The fruit flies have also discovered that you can eat the seeds and skin of some fruits, but not others. They are amazed by all the shapes and sizes of fruits.

Nicholas, Gracie, Jake, Ben, and Zak are thankful
for so many delicious fruits. Some day they hope
to have tasted every fruit in the world.

But most of all, they are grateful they could share fruit with friends.